The Blessed Virgin M[ary]	of Syracuse
St. Michael the Archa[ngel]	[St.] Nicholas
St. Gabriel the Archangel	St. Sylvester
St. John the Baptist	St. Jerome
St. John the Apostle	St. Brendan the Navigator
St. Peter the Apostle	St. Gregory the Great
St. Paul the Apostle	St. Fiacre
St. James the Apostle	St. Gobnait
St. Anne	St. Drogo of Sebourg
St. Cecilia	St. Robert of Newminster
St. Agnes	St. Francis of Assisi
St. Christopher	St. Hugh of Lincoln
St. Barbara	St. Juliana of Liège
St. Sebastian	St. Albert the Great
St. Margaret of Antioch	St. Thomas Aquinas and St. Anselm of Canterbury

© 2016 by Daniel Mitsui

All rights reserved. No part of this book may be used or reproduced in any manner whatsoever, except in the case of reprints in the context of reviews, without written permission from Ave Maria Press®, Inc., P.O. Box 428, Notre Dame, IN 46556, 1-800-282-1865.

Founded in 1865, Ave Maria Press is a ministry of the United States Province of Holy Cross.

www.avemariapress.com

Paperback: ISBN-13-978-1-59471-724-6

Cover and text design by Christopher D. Tobin.

Printed and bound in the United States of America.

Introduction

The images in this book are details from ink drawings that I made to illustrate the lives of saints. Some of the decorative borders and lettering are taken from other drawings and rearranged into the compositions here, but all of the artwork originally came from my own hand.

As an artist, my preference is to draw the lives of the saints from the Apostolic age, the age of the Fathers, and the Middle Ages. The task here is to construct an iconographic likeness of the holy man or woman—a different (and to me at least, more interesting) task than to represent a physical likeness known from photographs or portrait paintings.

When drawing saints who lived after Biblical times, I refer to the traditional hagiographies, those wonderful accounts of their miracle-filled lives. *The Golden Legend* is usually the first reference book that I pull off my shelf. It is a thirteenth-century encyclopedia of saints' lives compiled from liturgical lectionaries and patristic writings. It represents the entire tradition better than any other single book.

When I first read *The Golden Legend*, I was impressed by the enormous wealth of information, and by the intellectual seriousness with which its compiler, Blessed Jacobus de Voragine, approached his task. He readily admits when a story is based on a doubtful source, or when different versions of it exist. Yet his attitude to the hagiographies is generous; he gives them the benefit of the doubt whenever possible.

This starkly contrasts the attitude of so many Christians of modern times, which is derisive, dismissive, or at best patronizing. *It's cute*, they may say, *to draw St. Brendan celebrating Mass on the back of a whale, but of course we know that that didn't really happen.* Well, really? We do? What evidence is there against it? This is a very strange assertion for those who profess faith in an omnipotent God and in his revealed Word. No hagiography is stranger than the stories of the Old Testament and the stories of the New. What could be stranger than the resurrection of Jesus Christ?

Of course, the resurrection is an article of faith, something that a Christian is simply not permitted to disbelieve, and the words of the Old and New Testaments are inerrant; hagiographies are not (as Blessed Jacobus would be the first to admit). But our attitude toward the legends of the saints reveals and affects our attitude toward God, toward his creation, and toward his revelation.

We either live in a world in which these sorts of things happen, or we do not.

DANIEL MITSUI

The Blessed Virgin Mary, Mother of God, here holds a flower in one hand and her divine Son in the other. The Christ Child holds a goldfinch. The poses and attributes here are those of the Virgin of Antigua in Seville Cathedral. My drawing, however, is in a Chinese style, influenced by ink paintings, woodblock prints, and porcelain designs.

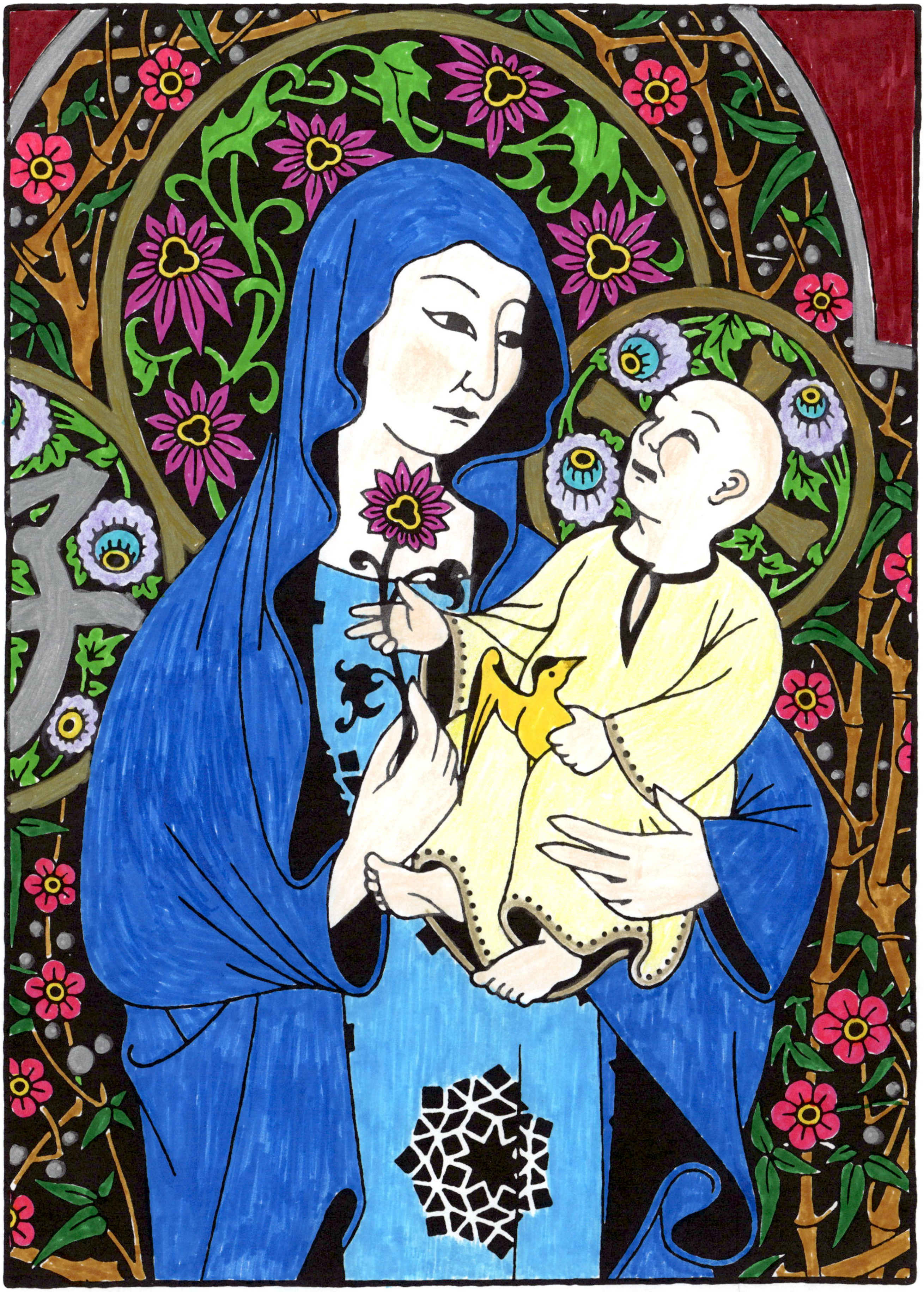

St. Michael the Archangel is one of the seven Archangels, and the prince of the heavenly host. To him God gave the task of expelling the rebellious Lucifer from heaven, of contesting with Satan over the body of Moses, of escorting the souls of the saints to heaven, and of defeating the dragon and his angels in battle during the End Times.

SANCTUS MICHEL

St. Gabriel the Archangel is the messenger of God, who is given the task of communicating divine messages to man. Here, he instructs St. Joseph in a dream to take the Blessed Virgin Mary and the Christ Child and to flee to Egypt to escape the Massacre of the Innocents. I drew this in the style of a Japanese woodblock print.

我が汝に告ぐ、まで彼處に居れ、はヘロデ孩兒を殺んとて之を索めんすればなり、と。

St. John the Baptist was the forerunner of Jesus Christ on Earth. After he was beheaded at Herod's order, St. John the Baptist's soul descended to the dead and was the forerunner of Jesus Christ in the Limbo of the Patriarchs. Tradition holds that he was sanctified in his mother's womb, at the Visitation, and that he will plead for mankind at the Last Judgment.

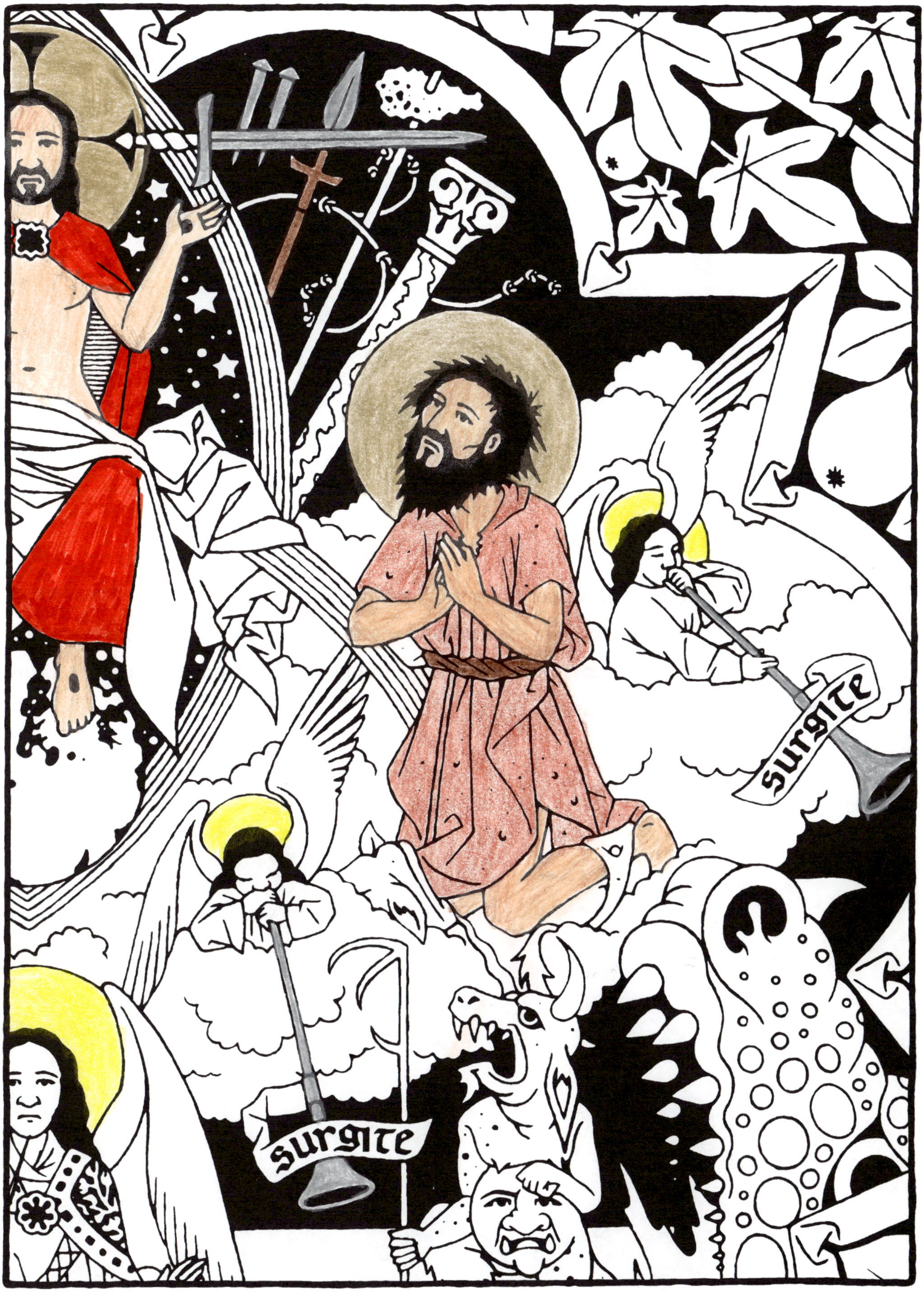
surgite
surgite

St. John the Apostle, Evangelist and Revelator, was the youngest Apostle and the only one to stand faithfully at the foot of the Cross. Tradition holds that he preached throughout Asia, survived being plunged into boiling oil, died in his ninety-ninth year, and was bodily assumed into heaven, leaving behind a tomb filled with manna.

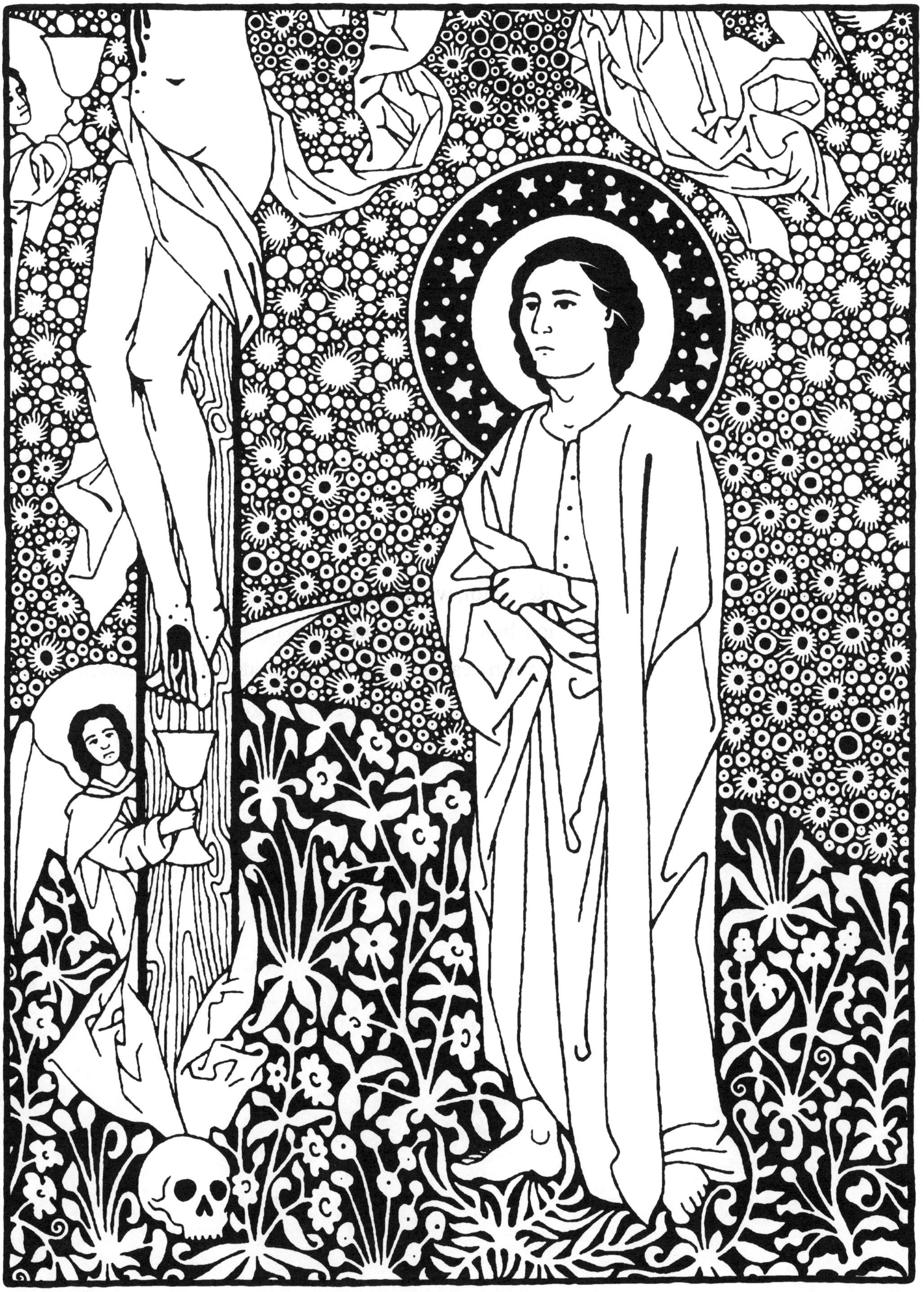

St. Peter the Apostle was chosen by Jesus Christ as the rock upon which Christ would build his Church. St. Peter served as Bishop of Antioch and then of Rome, contested with the sorcerer Simon Magus, and was crucified upside down under Roman Emperor Nero. Here I drew him walking upon the water to meet Jesus Christ, but sinking beneath the waves because of his doubt.

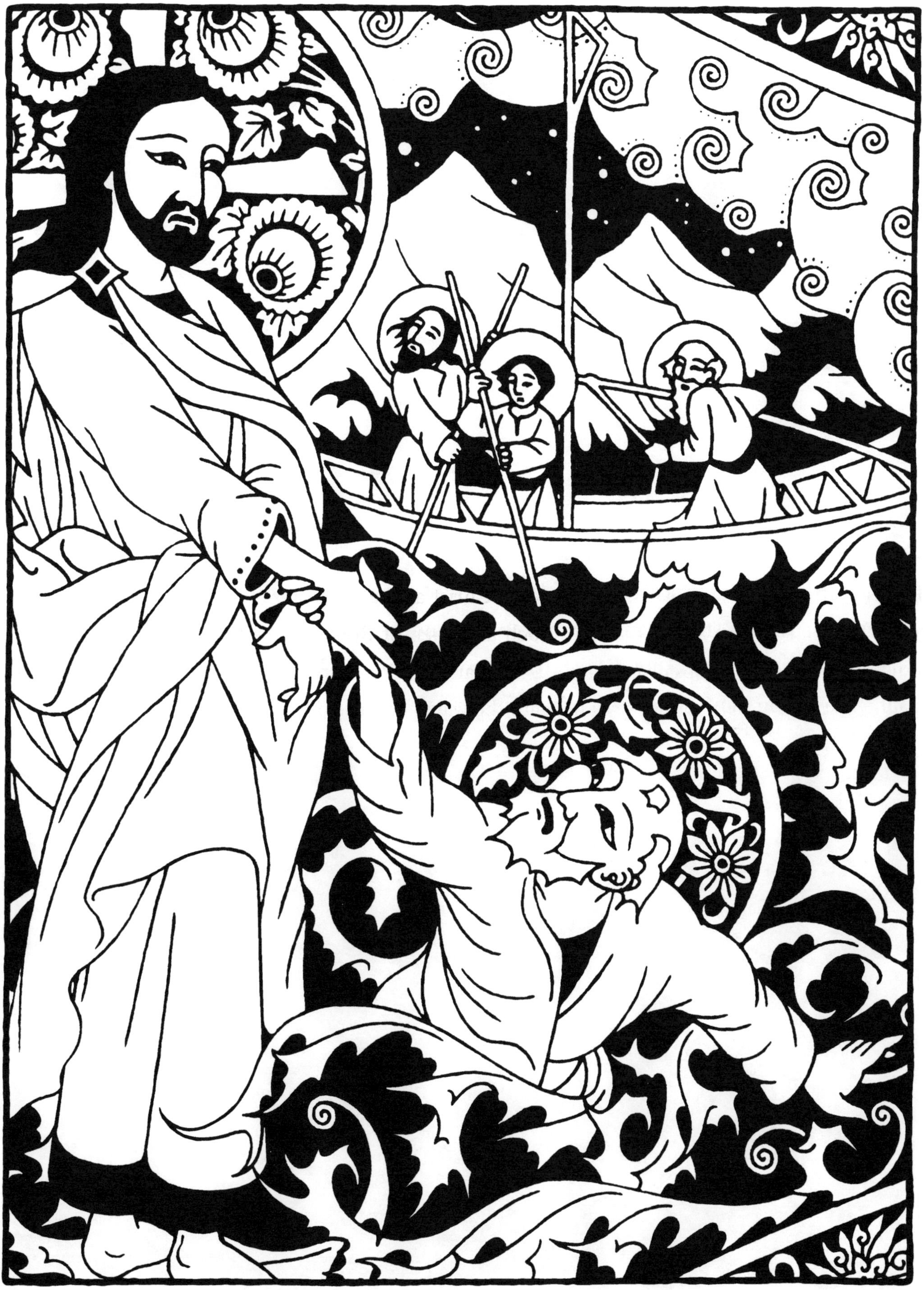

St. Paul the Apostle, once a zealous persecutor of Christians, was miraculously converted on the road to Damascus. His extensive missionary journeys and writings converted countless men and women, Gentiles and Jews, to Christianity. He was beheaded by sword at Nero's command. Along with St. Peter, St. Paul is the patron saint of the Roman Church.

SANCTAS

St. James the Apostle was present at the Transfiguration of Jesus Christ and the Agony in the Garden. He was the first of the Apostles to be martyred, beheaded by sword at Herod's command. Compostela, where St. James's relics are kept, has for centuries been a popular pilgrimage destination. For this reason, St. James is depicted here in pilgrim garb.

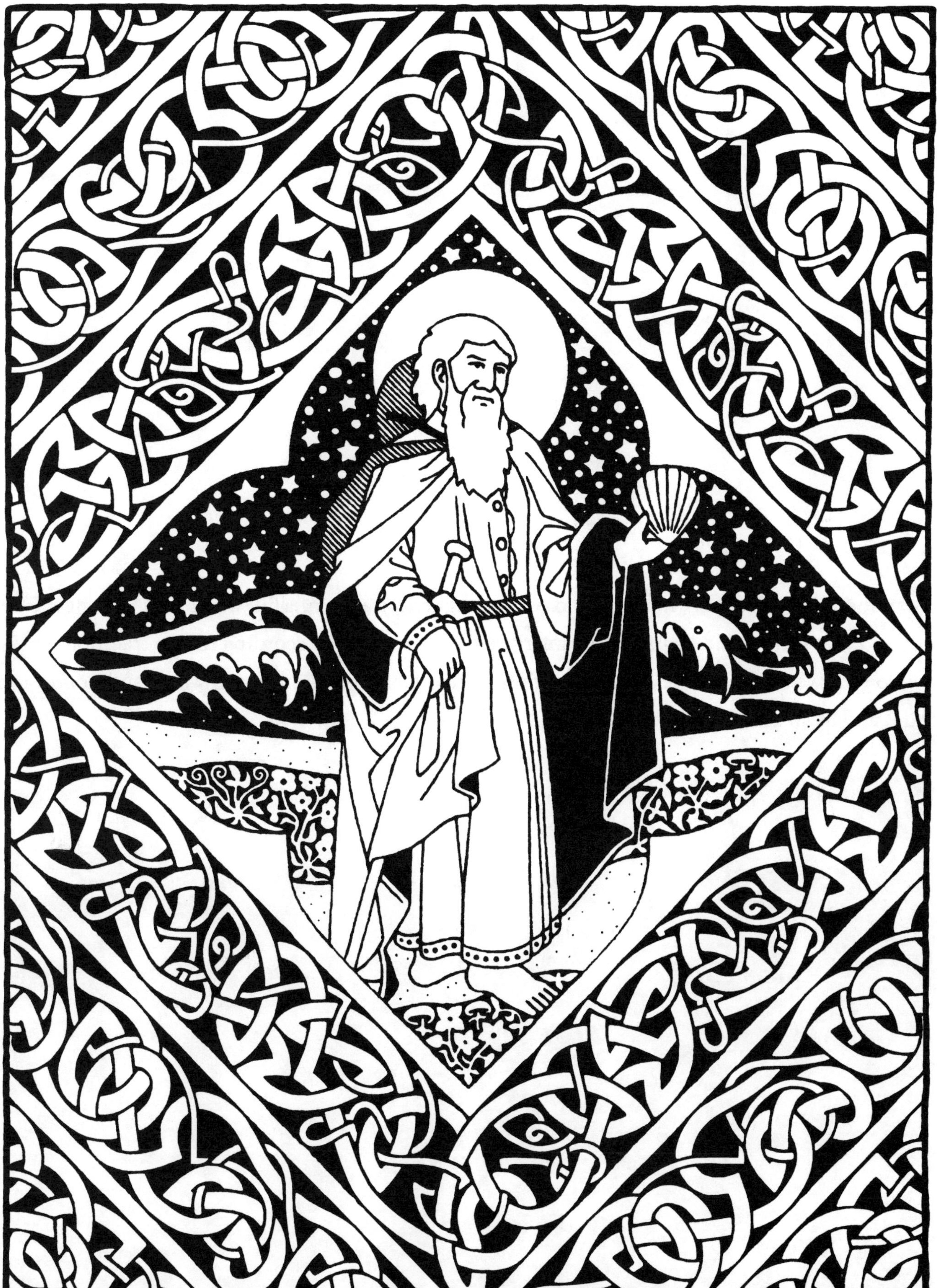

St. Anne and St. Joachim, her husband, were for twenty years infertile when the Archangel Gabriel announced that they would be parents of the Blessed Virgin Mary. According to one tradition, St. Anne was widowed two or three times, and through her second and third husbands was grandmother to five Apostles and St. Joseph the Just.

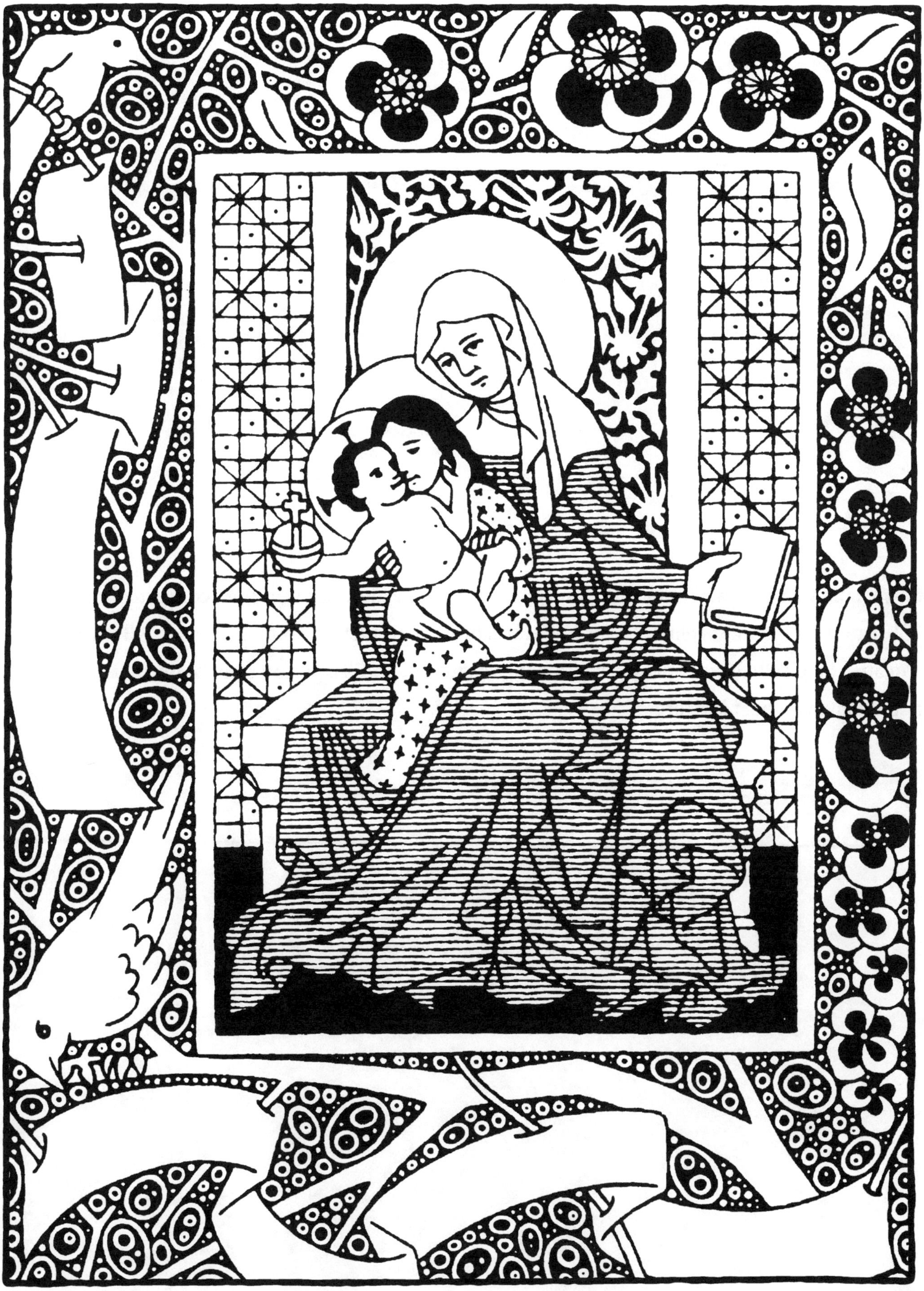

St. Cecilia was a Roman noblewoman who, immediately after her wedding, converted her husband to the Christian faith and to celibacy. Her husband's brother converted soon afterward. All three died martyrs' deaths. St. Cecilia's house was consecrated as a church. She is a patron saint of musicians, and is often depicted playing a portative organ.

S · CECILIA

St. Agnes was an early virgin martyr. After refusing to wed a pagan, she was arrested and subjected to abuse. A miraculous light protected her from her assailants. St. Agnes's suitor converted after being struck dead by this light and restored to life by her prayers. When she was thrown into a fire, the flames burned the hostile crowd instead.

SANCTA AGNES

St. Christopher was a giant man with a frightening face. Determined to put himself in the service of the world's most powerful ruler, he served first a human king, then the devil, and finally Jesus Christ. While carrying the Christ Child across a turbulent river, St. Christopher felt the entire weight of the world upon his shoulders. He died a martyr.

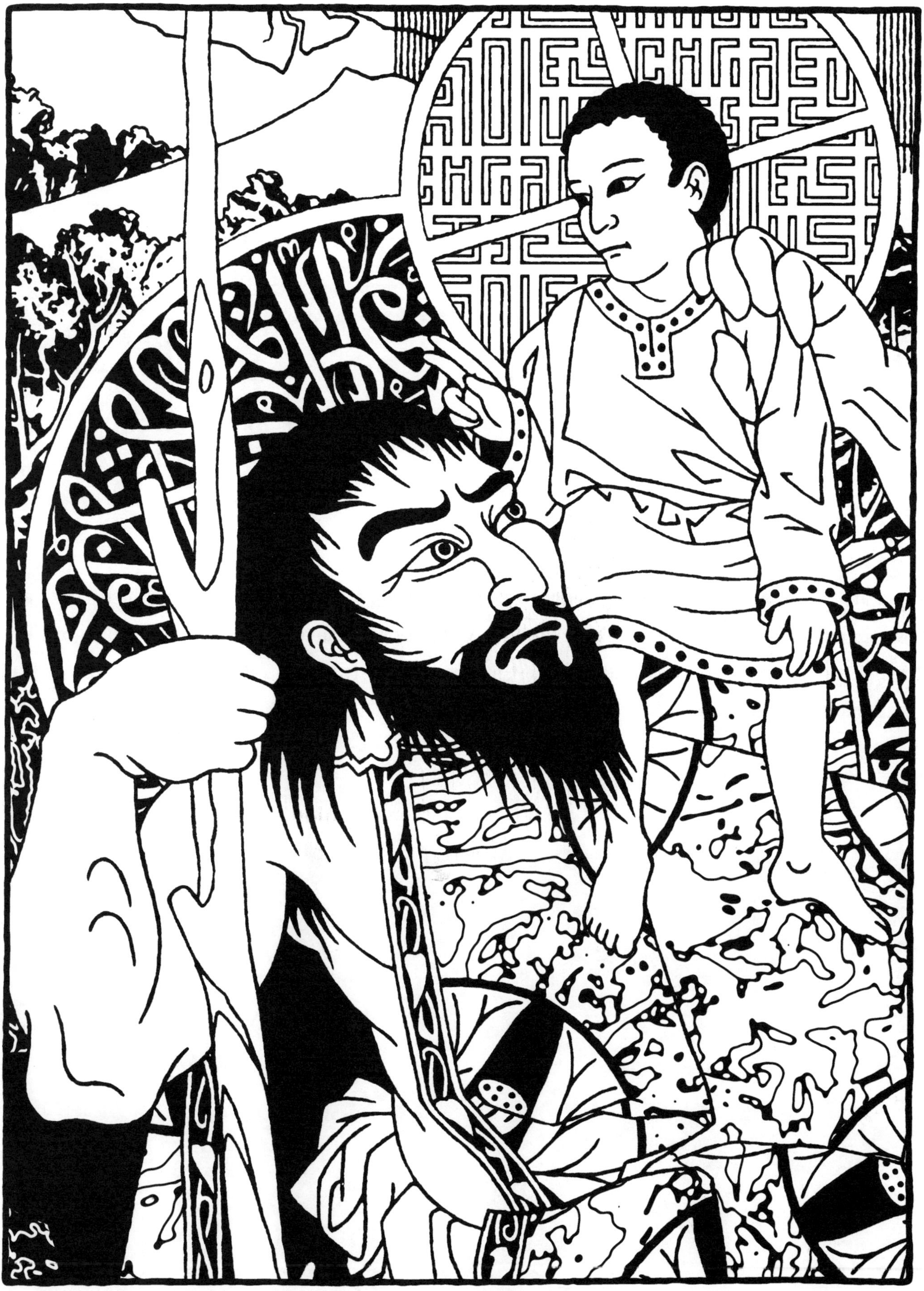

St. Barbara spent her youth living in a tower. After her conversion to Christianity, she ordered a third window be made in the tower to symbolize the Holy Trinity. Her pagan father was so enraged by this that he took her to a mountaintop and killed her. St. Barbara is a patron saint of protection against lightning, fire, and explosions.

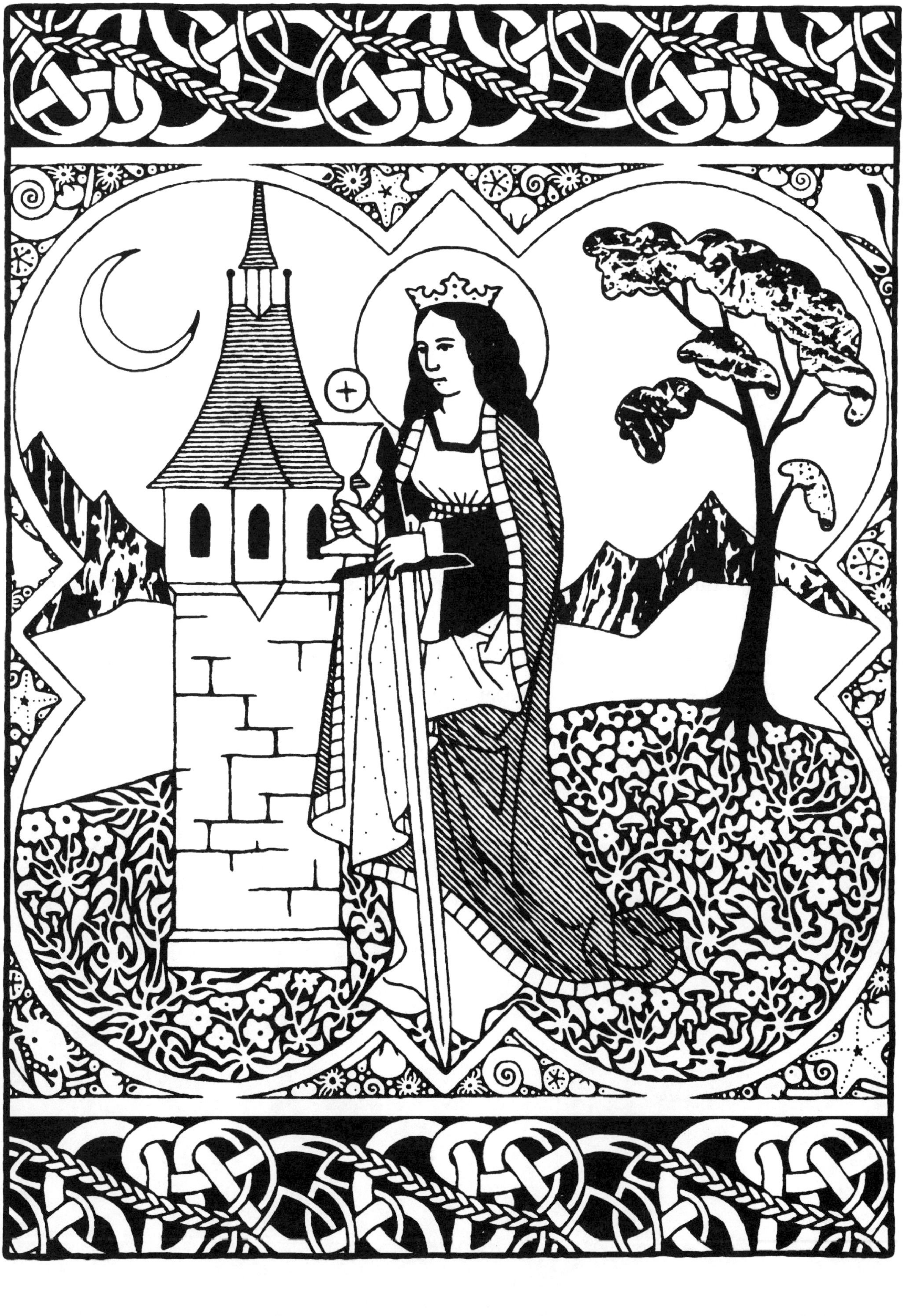

St. Sebastian was a third-century martyr. While an officer in the Roman army, he encouraged persecuted Christians to maintain their faith, won converts through miraculous cures, and destroyed more than two hundred pagan idols. In retribution, the Emperor Diocletian ordered him shot full of arrows. St. Sebastian survived the attempt, but was then beaten to death.

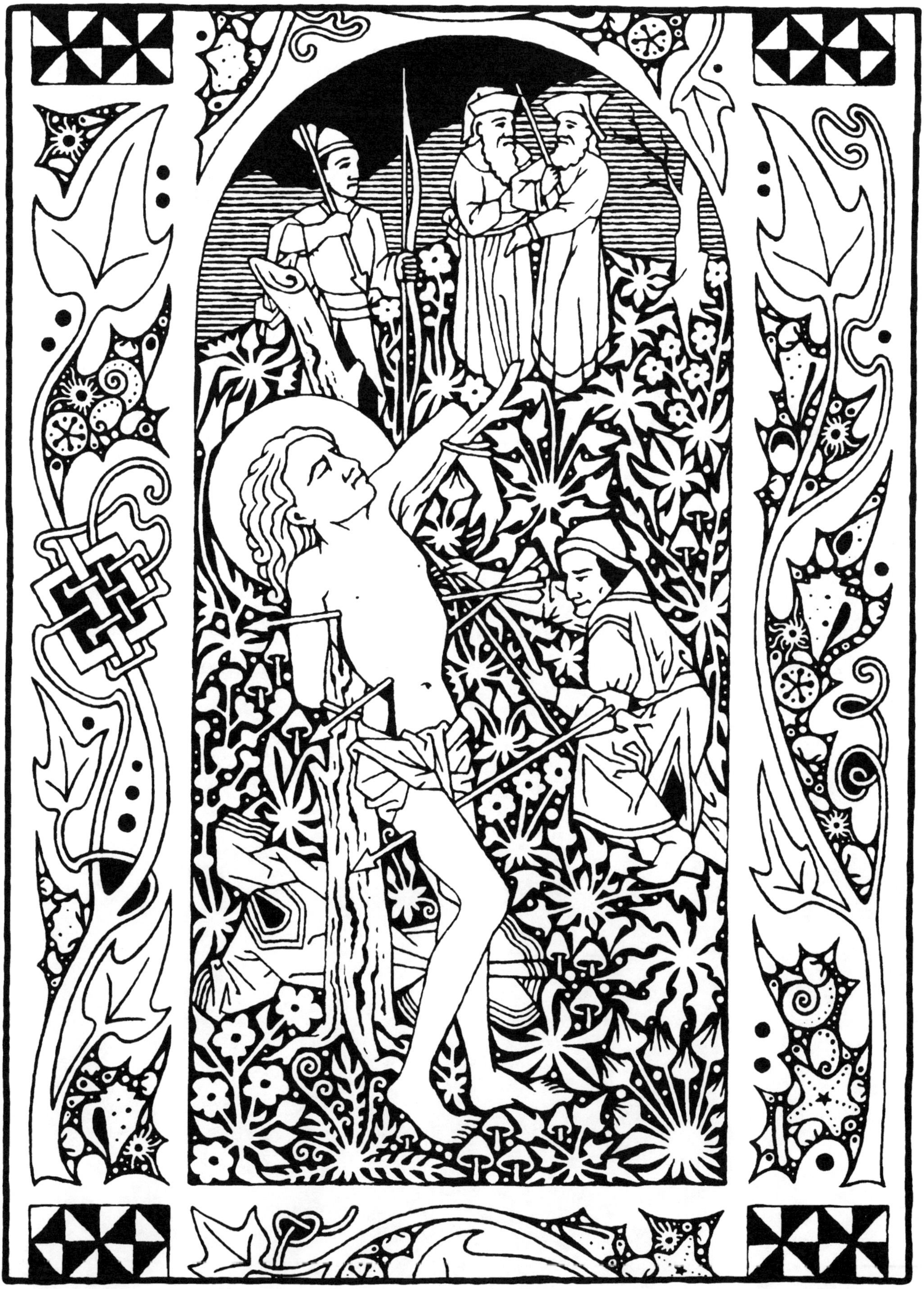

St. Margaret of Antioch refused marriage to a pagan official, who ordered her savagely beaten. A dragon appeared in her prison and swallowed her, but when she made the Sign of the Cross the dragon burst open and she emerged unharmed. She survived also being burned and boiled, but was at last martyred by decapitation.

MARGARET OF ANTIOCH

St. Lucy of Syracuse gave her wealth to the poor, which so angered her betrothed that he denounced her to the pagan consul. Condemned to torture and death after refusing to sacrifice to idols, St. Lucy was set on fire and pierced through the throat, yet remained alive until she was able to receive Holy Communion a final time.

SANCTA
LVCIA

St. Nicholas was born in the late third century, and demonstrated extraordinary piety, generosity, and miracle-working while yet a child. He was ordained Bishop of Myra, suffered imprisonment under Diocletian, and attended the Council of Nicea. St. Nicholas restored to life three boys who had been kidnapped and butchered during a famine.

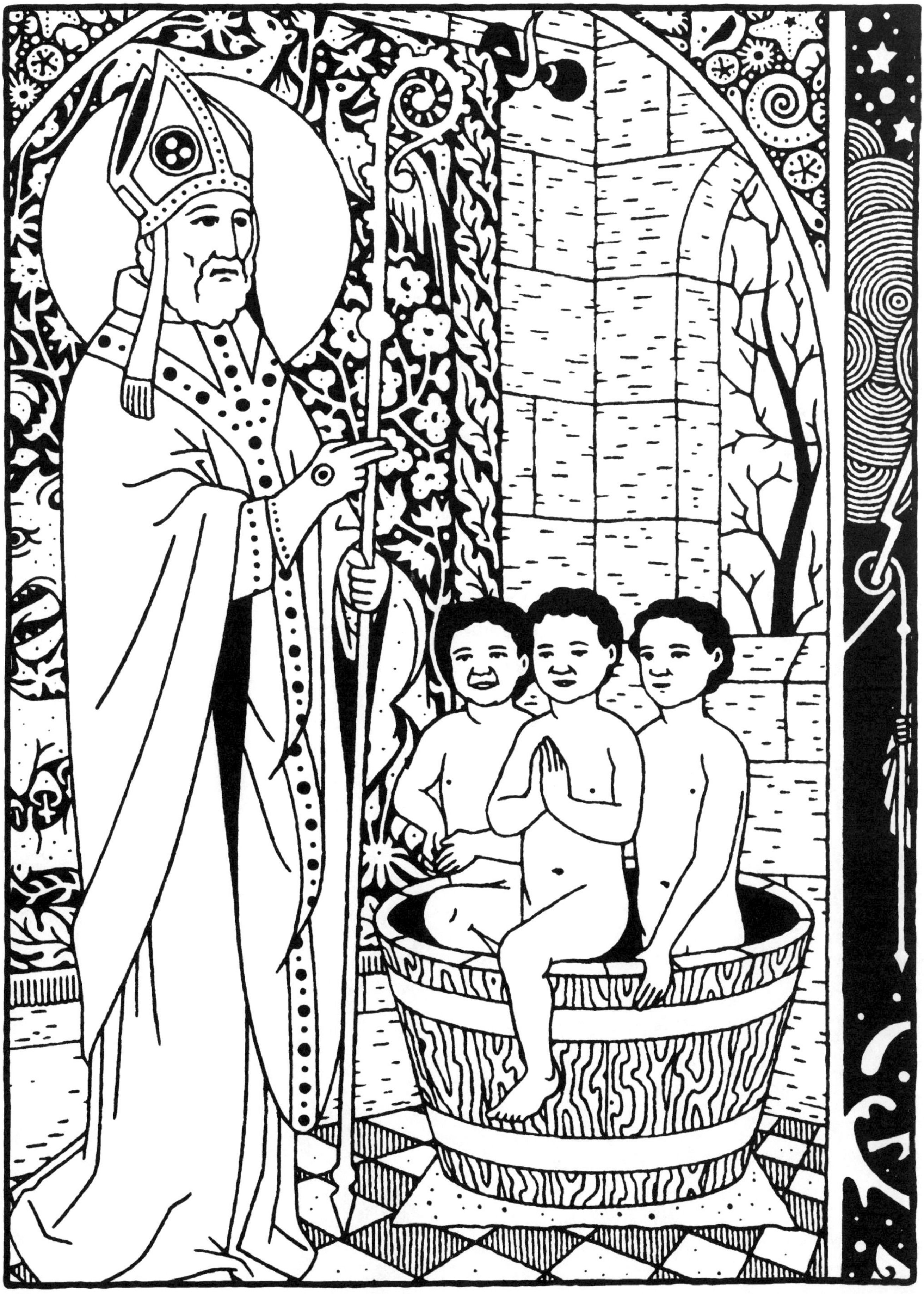

St. Sylvester was a pope of the early fourth century. His reign began about the time of the conversion of the Emperor Constantine to Christianity. By some accounts, St. Sylvester had a role in that conversion. He publicly debated Jewish scholars on matters of theology and muzzled a dragon that was spewing its poisonous breath into the air of Rome.

Sancte Silvester

ora pro nobis

St. Jerome, a great scholar and polemicist, lived in the late fourth and early fifth centuries. He spent many years as a hermit, translated the Bible into Latin, and founded a monastic community in Bethlehem. Because he was a priest of the Diocese of Rome, he is depicted in art as a cardinal. He is accompanied by a lion that he befriended.

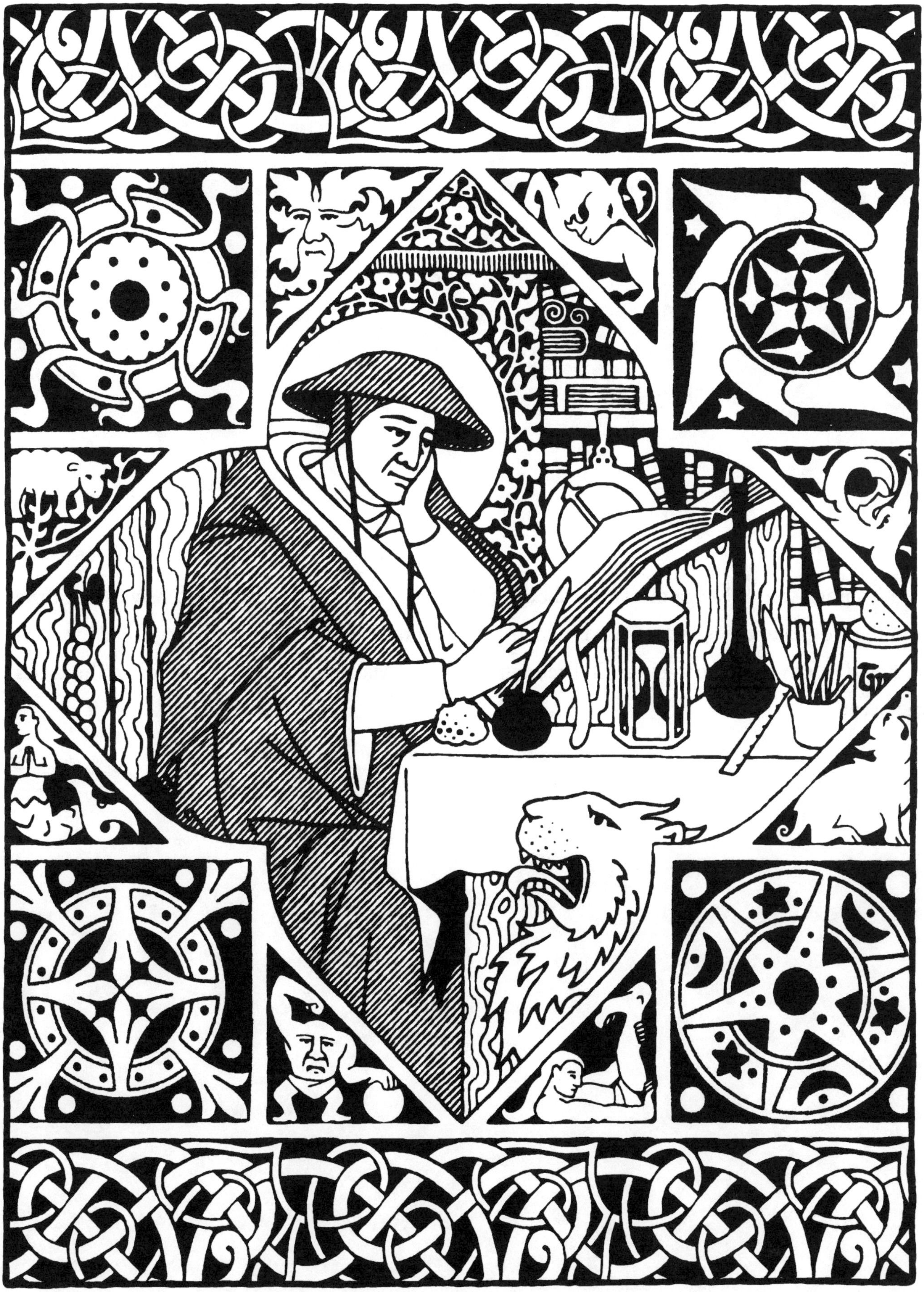

St. Brendan the Navigator was an abbot of the sixth century who made extensive sea journeys to spread the Gospel to the islands around Ireland. His most famous adventures are recounted in the *Voyage of St. Brendan*. On several occasions, St. Brendan celebrated Mass on the back of Iasconius, the largest fish in the ocean.

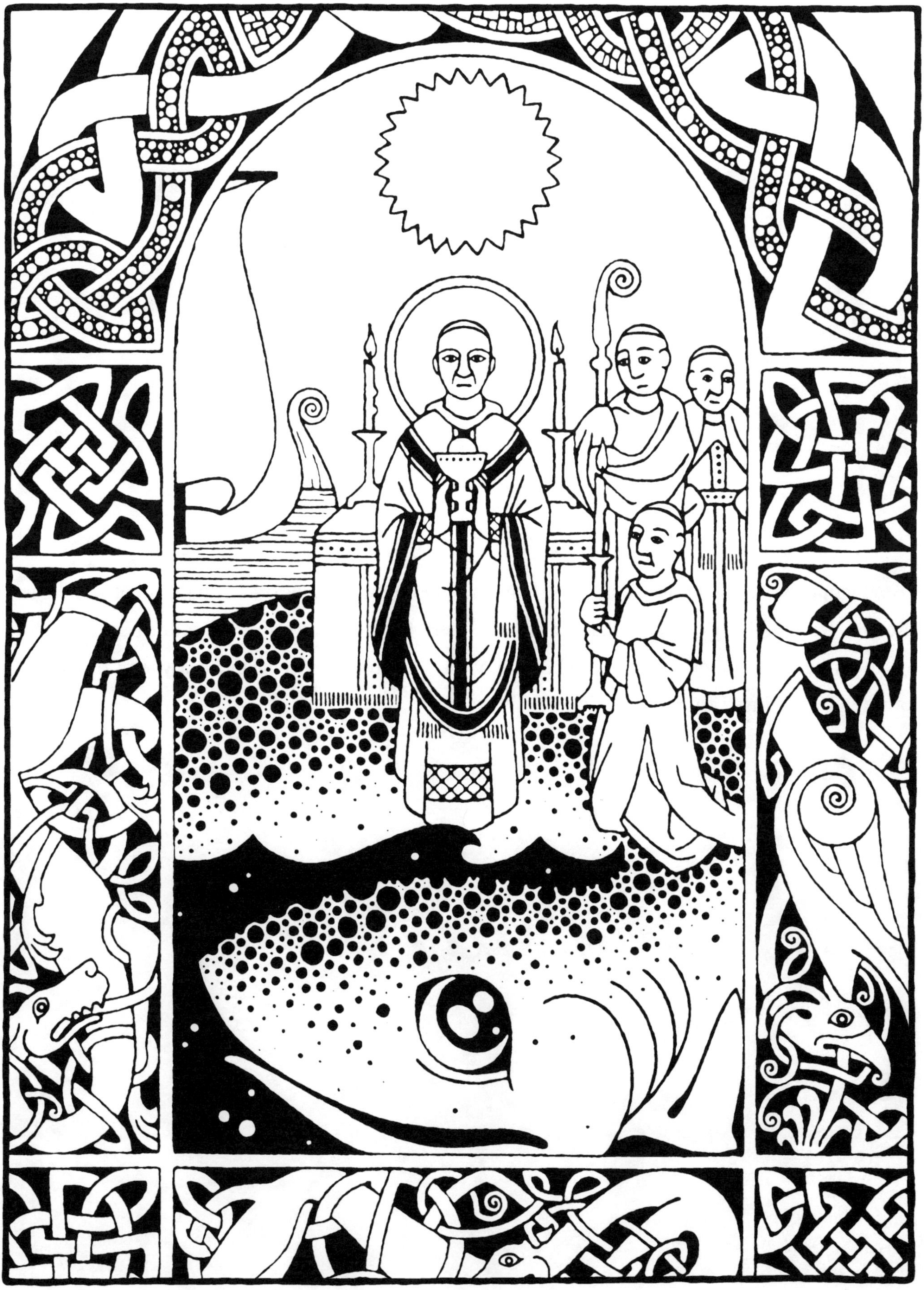

St. Gregory the Great reigned as pope from AD 590 to 604. He wrote brilliant theological treatises, codified the Roman liturgy and its music, and promoted the spirituality and discipline of the Benedictine Order, to which he belonged. While celebrating Mass, St. Gregory experienced a vision of Jesus Christ surrounded by the instruments of his Passion.

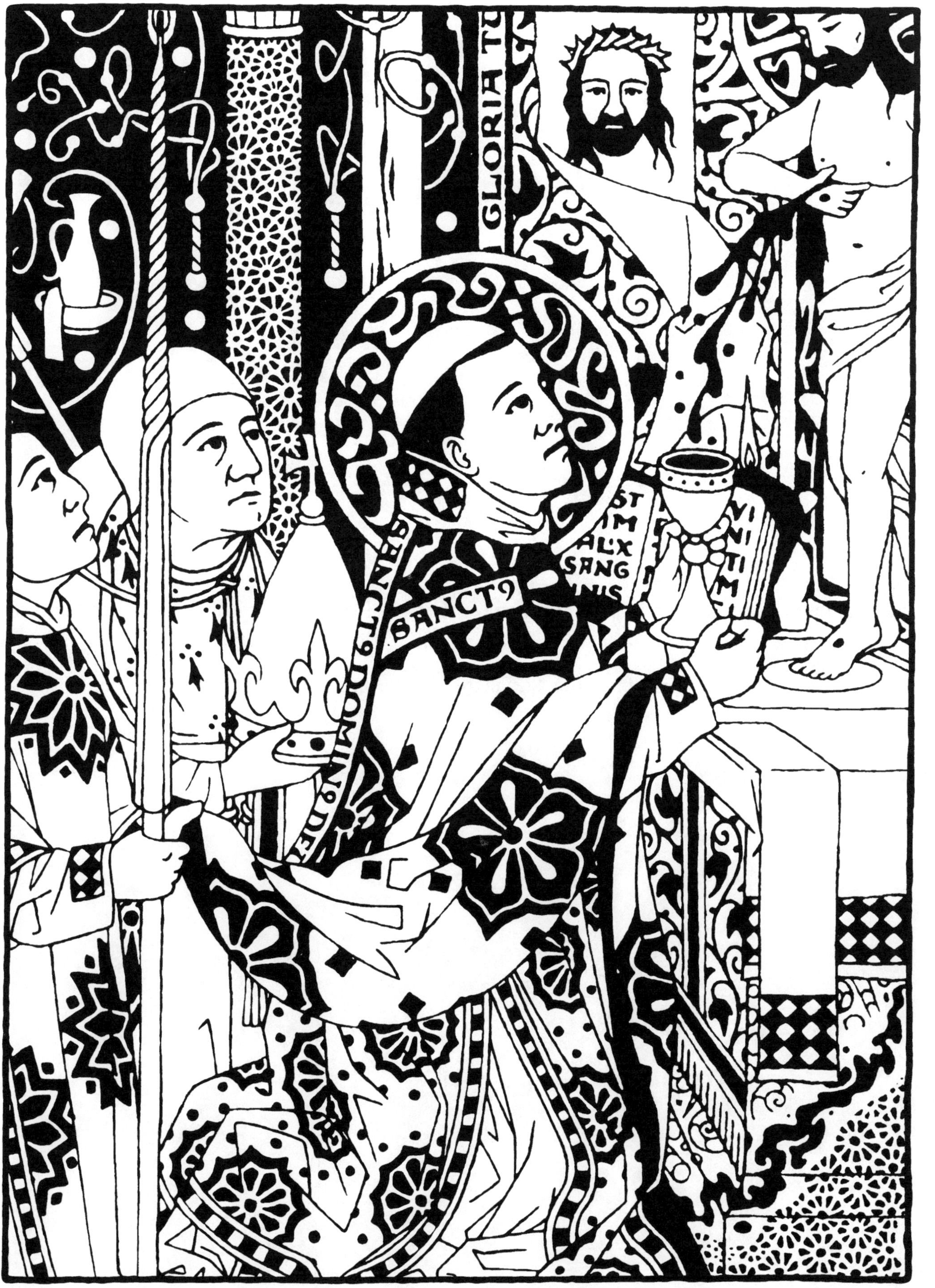
GLORIA TU
SANCT9

St. Fiacre was a seventh-century hermit who was born in Ireland and settled in northern France. He miraculously ploughed the tract of land upon which he built his hermitage with the point of his staff. He possessed extraordinary powers of healing. St. Fiacre is a patron saint of gardeners and chauffeurs.

TVLIT
ERGOD
OMINV
SDEVS
HOMIN
EMETP
OSVITE
VMINP
ARADIS
OVOLV

St. Gobnait was an Irish abbess of the sixth century. She founded her abbey on a spot revealed to her by the miraculous presence of nine white deer. She is a patron saint of beekeeping; the bees kept by her nuns once saved the abbey by attacking a band of marauders. I included nine white deer, four honeybees, and a hive in my drawing.

S HOBUAIT NAOFA

St. Drogo of Sebourg lived in the twelfth century. He spent his youth on pilgrimage and shepherding, at times bilocating to attend Mass while watching his flocks. He developed a physical infirmity and spent the last forty years of his life in a hermit's cell attached to his parish church. St. Drogo is a patron saint of shepherds and of coffeehouses.

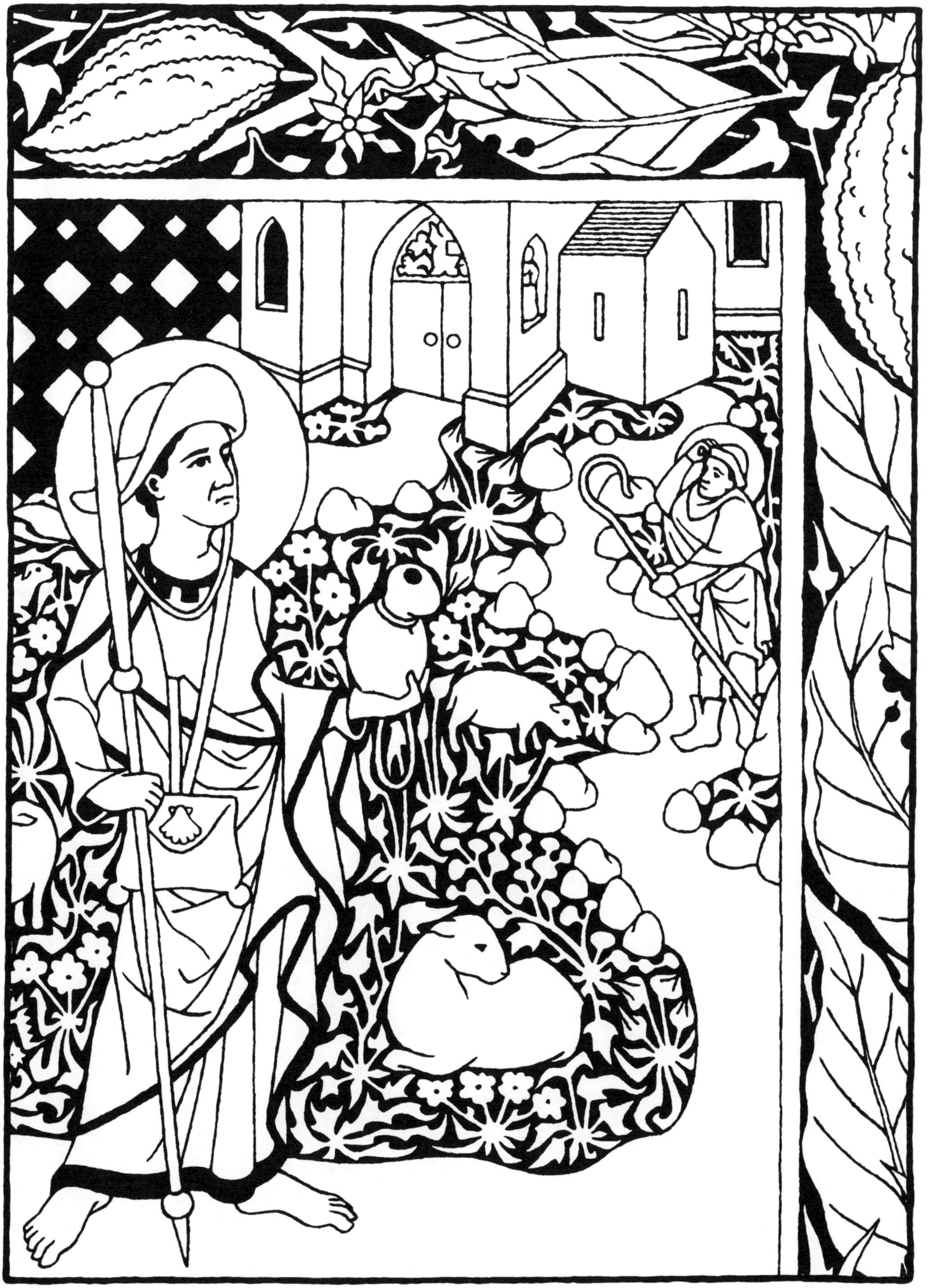

St. Robert of Newminster was a twelfth-century Cistercian abbot. He was renowned for his fleshly mortification and his power over malevolent spirits. In this image, the four shields represent the Abbey of Newminster and three other monasteries founded by the saint; I wrote the dates of their foundations in Cistercian numerals.

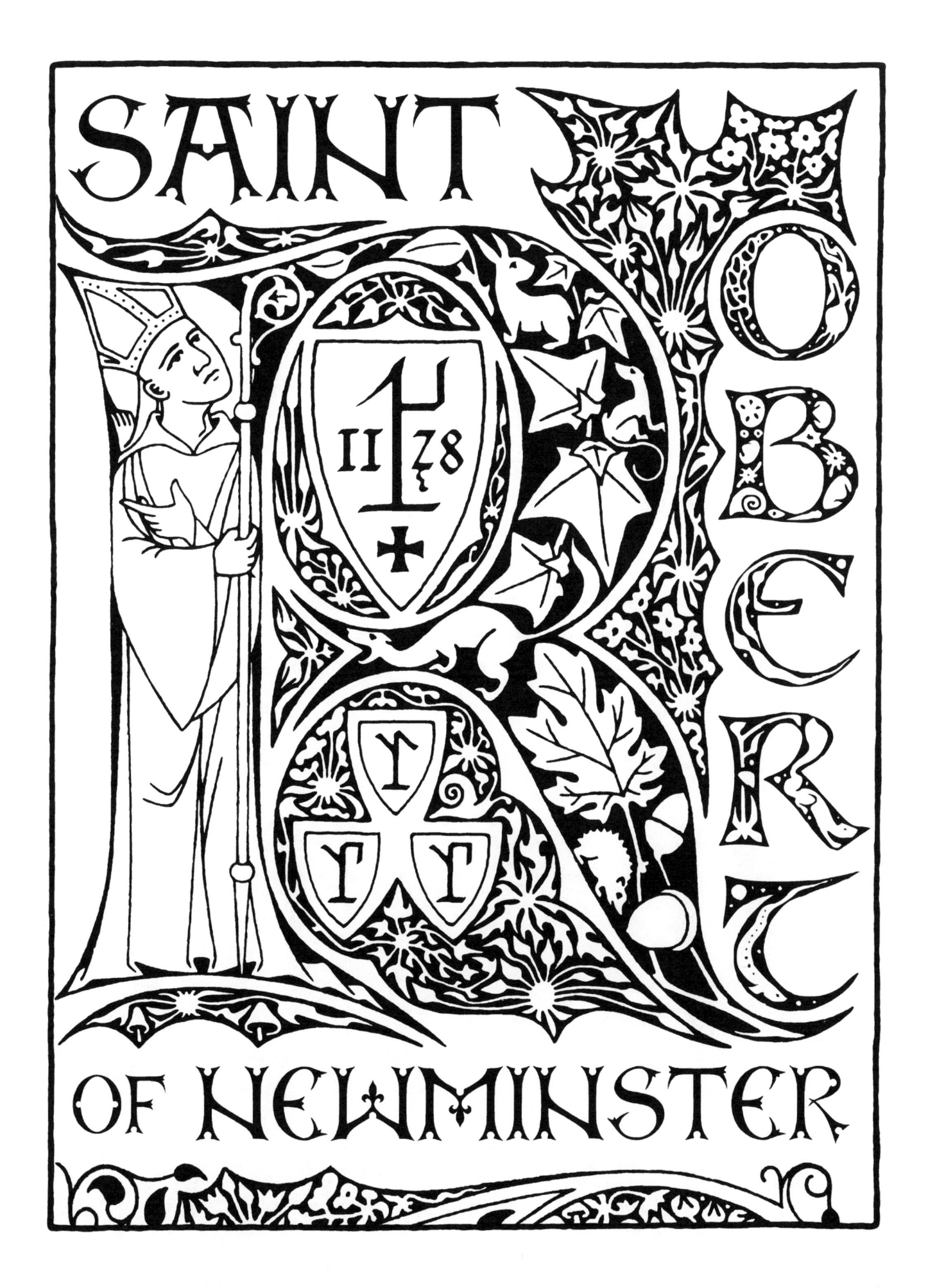

SAINT ROBERT OF NEWMINSTER

St. Francis of Assisi is honored for his love of poverty, his communion with the animal world, and his bearing of the stigmata. He founded the Franciscan Order in the first decade of the thirteenth century. I drew St. Francis rebuking a novice who wanted to own private property, and pacifying a wolf that terrorized the town of Gubbio.

SANCTE FRANCISCE

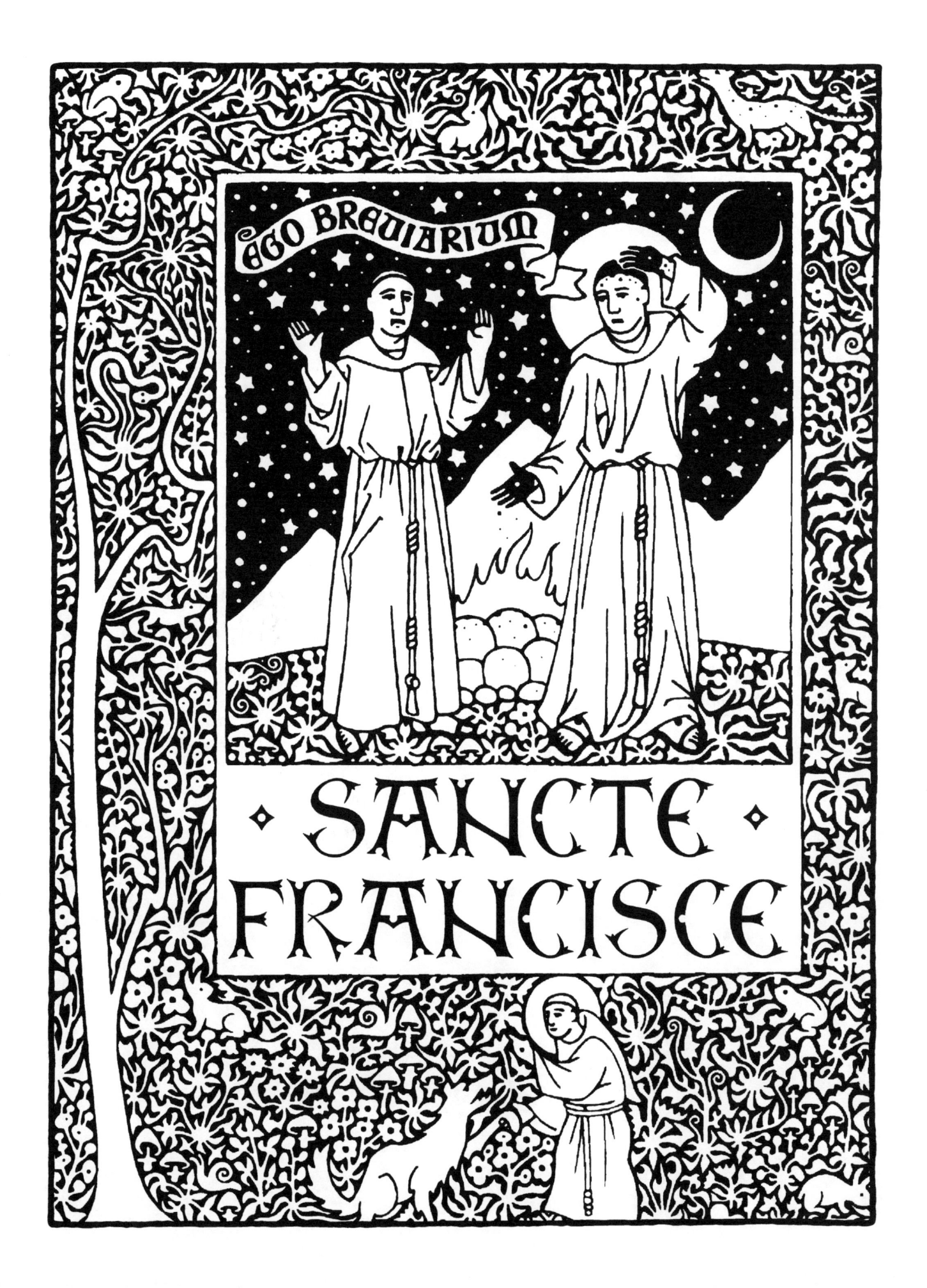

St. Hugh of Lincoln was a twelfth-century Carthusian hermit who became the Bishop of Lincoln. He oversaw the rebuilding of the city's cathedral choir after an earthquake in 1185; the resulting edifice contains some of the most beautiful Gothic architecture in England. A swan befriended the bishop, ate from his hand, and guarded him while he slept.

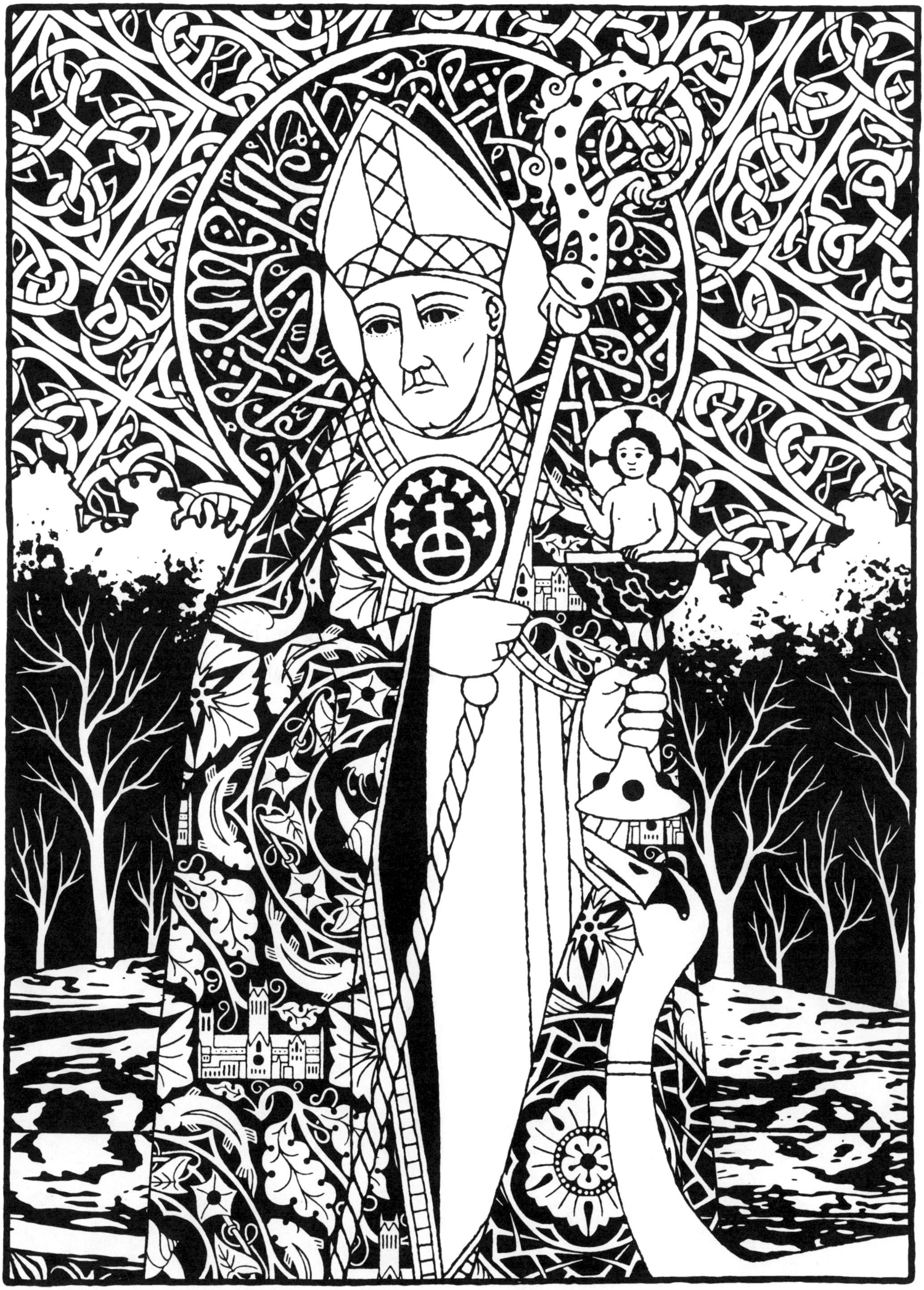

St. Juliana of Liège was a thirteenth-century Premonstratensian canoness regular. She experienced a mystical vision of the full moon with a dark blemish, representing the liturgical year and its lack of a feast especially in honor of the Holy Eucharist. This vision led to the establishment of the feast of Corpus Christi.

Laureata plebs fi

St. Albert the Great was a thirteenth-century Dominican friar, bishop, philosopher, and natural scientist. His efforts helped to legitimate the study of nature within the Christian intellectual tradition. I drew St. Albert seated at his desk, writing, surrounded by his books, bottles, instruments of calculation, and devotional objects.

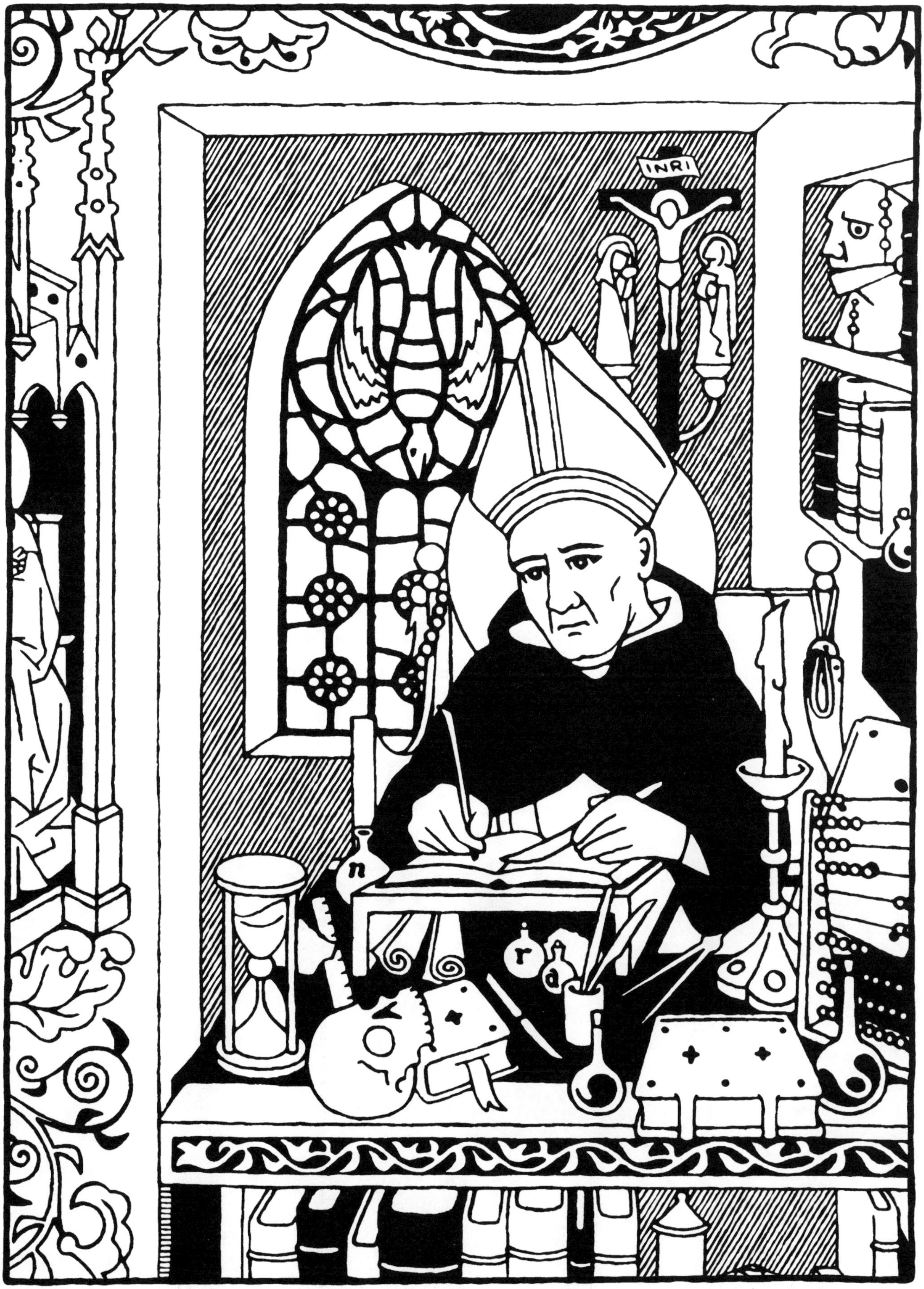
INRI
n
r
a

St. Thomas Aquinas and St. Anselm of Canterbury were two of the most celebrated thinkers of the Middle Ages. St. Thomas, author of the *Summa Theologica* and the *Summa Contra Gentes*, integrated Aristotelean philosophy into Christian thought. St. Anselm, a bishop of the twelfth century, is considered the founder of Scholasticism.

FIDES QᴇRᴇNS INELLECTUM

Artist Daniel Mitsui specializes in ink drawing. His meticulously detailed creations—created entirely by hand on paper or vellum—are held in collections worldwide. Since his baptism into the Catholic Church in 2004, he has focused most of his art on religious subjects.

Mitsui is a 2004 graduate of Dartmouth College (cum laude and senior fellow), where he studied drawing, oil painting, etching, lithography, wood carving, bookbinding, and film animation.

The Vatican commissioned Mitsui to illustrate a new edition of the Roman Pontifical in 2011. In 2012, he established Millefleur Press, an imprint for publishing fine books and broadsides of his artwork and typography. He is a prolific designer of custom bookplates.

Born in Georgia and raised in Illinois, Mitsui lives in Chicago with his wife, Michelle, and their three children.